COPYRIGHT NOTICE

Copyright © 2020 by Arthur Mitchell III of artmitch.com. All rights reserved. You are welcome to print a copy of this document for your personal use. Other than that, no part of this publication may be reproduced, stored, or transmitted in any form or by any means, electronic, mechanical, photocopying, recording, scanning, or otherwise, except as permitted under Section 107 or 108 of the 1976 United States Copyright Act, without the prior written permission of the author.

Requests to the author and publisher for permission should be addressed to the following email:
zajinspirations@gmail.com

6 Tips to Cope with Having a Disability

TABLE OF CONTENTS

TIP 1: ACCEPTING WHO YOU ARE

TIP 2: MAKING ADJUSTMENTS

TIP 3: TAKE CONTROL OF YOUR DAY

TIP 4: PERSONAL DEVELOPMENT

TIP 5: CREATE HOBBIES

TIP 6: SURROUND YOURSELF WITH LIKE MINDED PEOPLE

ARTHUR MITCHELL, A.K.A ART MITCH, HAS BEEN INVOLVED WITH YOUTH FOR OVER TEN YEARS, BY HELPING YOUTH BUILD CONFIDENCE, INSPIRING CHANGE AND TRANSFORMING LIVES.

THROUGH HIS YEARS OF VOLUNTEERING WITH VARIOUS YOUTH ORGANIZATIONS, ART MITCH HAS BEEN IMPACTING YOUTH ACROSS THE GLOBE.

BEING DIAGNOSED AT THE AGE OF 6 WAS DIFFICULT BUT HE DIDN'T ALLOW IT TO STOP HIM FROM ACHIEVING. HIS MISSION, IS TO PUT IT ALL TOGETHER AND TELL THE WORLD HOW HE IS OVERCOMING.

THANK YOU SO MUCH FOR TAKING TIME TO LEARN HOW HE COPED WITH HIS DISABILITY!

TIP 1: ACCEPTING WHO YOU ARE!!!

Why am I like this? Why do I look like this? Why did this happen to me? These are just some of the questions I asked myself. I was diagnosed at the age of 6 with Keratoconus, which is an eye disease that causes my vision to be blurry. See, I never had a normal childhood. Life for me as a kid became difficult when I was diagnosed. After some years, I had to learn how to accept the fact that I had a disability.

I couldn't do anything about it but to live in it and grow through it. Yes, having a disability is hard and at times is depressing. The sooner you acknowledge the disability and understand you are still somebody, the greater your life will be. Wake up every day with a I Am attitude.

I want you to repeat this daily; I AM great, I AM confident, and I AM intelligent. Watch how your words will command your day.

No matter what, I AM.
~Arthur Mitchell.

CHOOSE YOUR DAY!

Write down a thought you are currently having and why.

_____

_____

What is one affirmation you can use to help you move from negative to positive?

_____

Write it below on each line and say it aloud.

_____

_____

_____

_____

TIP 2: MAKING THE ADJUSTMENTS

Can you imagine 6 years old and having something on your face to wear just to be able to see. Not just any glasses but ones with a very strong prescription due to my vision. I took one step and almost fell they were so thick. This was an adjustment I would have to make in order to see.

Making adjustments can sometimes be uncomfortable and hurt at times but in life we are going to have to make them. Another great example is when Michael Jordan came back from retirement he wasn't the same as he was before so, he had to make some adjustments to get back in the game. For him this meant practicing harder, shooting more shots, and running more.

What are some adjustments that you can make to help you cope with what you are going through? In the next few chapters you will see the strategies I used to help me cope with my disability, Keratoconus.

Adjustments are not to discomfort you, its to make you better in the long run
~Arthur Mitchell

Arthur Mitchell

ASSESS AND ADJUST!!!

Situation:

___

Positve thought:

___

What adjustment can you make today?

___

TIP 3: TAKE CONTROL OF YOUR DAY

My bible says "Death and life are in the power of the tongue". That means you have the power to speak how good your day will be or you can speak how negative your day will be. the choice is yours. I know sometimes we wake up thinking; I am going to have a bad day, I am not normal, People are looking at me funny, The same things are going to keep happening to me, and What the heck. I too was in that head space.

When I had my last corneal transplant it was the worst I ever had. I almost died under the anesthesia because I stopped breathing. To top it off my vision still wasn't clear. Coming out of a situation like that I felt horrible. I just knew life was over and I wasn't speaking about it but I was thinking it. I felt like I had no support which allowed depression to kick in and all I wanted to do was sleep. I asked my wife one day, "Why is this happening to me" and as soon as I uttered that question aloud I broke down crying. It was that day that made me take control of my life.

My coach always say "Don't let the way you feel affect the way you flow". For me this means yes I have a disability and yes my life is different but I have the power to control my day by the words I speak.

Everyday won't be perfect, but you have the power to control it.
~Arthur Mitchell

DECLARATIONS

MY DAY WILL BE:

MY FAMILY WILL BE:

MY CAREER WILL BE:

MY LIFE WILL BE:

TIP 4: PERSONAL DEVELOPMENT

My wife and I joined a MLM company years ago where we used to sell products. At first we were having much success and life was pretty dope. Then all of sudden, it stopped, nobody wanted anything we sold. I used to wake up days depressed, sad, and wondering where did the clients go? One of my team members asked me during a call were we doing our personal development? At the time I knew nothing about personal development. I would get up, read and pray, but that was it. When he explained it to me it changed my life forever, not only in my business but also dealing with Keratoconus as well. It was getting harder and harder waking up wearing glasses and still couldn't see. Scared to go outside at night because you thought you would run into something or better yet drive at night in fear of hitting somebody.

According to skillsyouneed.com, Personal development is a lifelong process. It is a way for people to assess their skills and qualities, consider their aims in life and set goals in order to realise and maximise their potential. This was an essential part of my journey because I would have lost my mind if I didn't add this to my everyday regimen. I realized that personal development wasn't one particular thing it could be words of affirmation, quotes of the day, bible verses, videos, and anything that kept you thinking positive.

My daily routine goes like this. I wake up at 5 am to pray and read my bible verse. I always give God his first. Then either listen to an audio via youtube or podcast. They say your mood is set by what you put in your mind first thing in the morning. The key to personal development is not doing this only in the morning but throughout the day so you can stay in that positive head space all day.

When your mind matches your destiny, anything is possible.
~Arthur Mitchell

PERSONAL DEVELOPMENT PLANNER

Personal development ideas

My Schedule

What time and days will you add personal development?

TIP 5:
CREATE A HOBBY

When I was younger, I went to this facility called the Boys and Girls Club. It was a place where kids of all ages would come together and do fun activities. I loved playing pool which I mastered due to playing so much. It became something that kept me focused and at peace. Find that one thing that gives you a way to help you release some of the stress you deal with daily. Game systems such as Atari, Sega, and Nintendo were some other hobbies I took part in to put my mind in a positive space.

Another great hobby is journaling. Writing about how your day has been going or what your going through helps you deal with the many emotions you may experience along your journey. What are your hobbies that has helped you cope through your disability?

When you create good habits, good things will happen to you.
~Arthur Mitchell

HOBBY
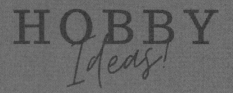

PICK THREE TO IMPLEMENT EACH WEEK?

Watching TV	Listening to music	Cooking	Arts and Crafts
Gardening	Painting	Listening to podcasts	Making music
Drawing	Baking	Coding	Playing a musical instrument
Reading books	Playing video games	Writing	Photography
Knitting	Acting	Playing sports	Dancing

TIP 6: SURROUND YOURSELF WITH LIKE MINDED PEOPLE

Have you ever had or knew of a crew that was always together. I mean ate lunch together, had classes together, and even graduated together. Well, I had that all throughout high school but as I got older I matured and needed to be around like-minded people.

I was at the point in my life where I had goals and I wanted to be around people who were goal oriented. I ended up joining this community and it blew my mind. They talked about mind, balance, health, and wealth. Being around them helped me step my game up and to also get focused on my goals.

I learned that having a disability, is something you shouldn't have to deal with on your own. Surrounding yourself around people that's going to motivate and encourage you through this process is key. Research groups or organizations that provide the support you need to overcome. What I found out is that not only did I need them but they needed me. In the event you cant find one do not hesitate to seek therapy. Sometimes talking to someone you don't know can help you more than you think.

Community builds Friendships which also builds Stability.
~Arthur Mitchell

MY COMMUNITY CONNECTIONS

List the organizations/resources in my community.

Contact information for each.

Date/time of my first meeting or encounter.

What did I learn from the expierence?

CHALLENGE

How many of you all remember the story of the tortoise and hare? A little refresher the hare challenged the tortoise to a race and he took the challenge knowing that he the hare was faster. So as the race partakes the hare took off and the turtle moved slow and steady. Even though the hare was faster the turtle never stopped and eventually won the race.

I told you that story my friend to let you know this journey we are on is a process. It is an everyday commitment to yourself to learn how to accept who you are, make adjustments, implement personal development, to take control of your day, to create hobbies, and surrounding yourself around like minded people.

I challenge you when you have those days where your not having such a good day to revert back to this book. Reevaluate the situation and make adjustments where needed. I can promise you things will not always feel as low as you may feel. There will be one day were you will be able to tell your story and encourage others.

Arthur Mitchell

Notes

Services

STAFF SUCCESS & PROFESSIONAL DEVELOPMENT

MENTORING SESSIONS

KEYNOTE SPEAKER

stay in touch

 AJINSPIRATIONS@MAIL.COM

 SUCCESSWITHARTHUR

  ARTHUR MITCHELL